To Anne Delvaux

PAUL DELVAUX

GRAPHIC WORK

FIFTY SPECIAL COPIES OF THIS BOOK, NUM-
BERED FROM 1 to 50, HAVE BEEN PUBLISHED.
EACH COPY INCLUDES TWO ORIGINAL,
SIGNED AND NUMBERED WIDE-MARGIN
LITHOGRAPHS — *REFLECTION* AND *THE
SPEECH*. ONE HUNDRED COPIES OF THESE
LITHOGRAPHS WERE RUN OFF, THE COPIES
NUMBERED FROM 1 to 50 BEING RESERVED
FOR INCLUSION IN THIS BOOK.

PAUL DELVAUX

GRAPHIC WORK

PREFACE, NOTES AND CATALOGUE

BY

MIRA JACOB

RIZZOLI
NEW YORK

French-language edition:
© 1976 by Mira Jacob, Paris and Éditions André Sauret, Monaco

English translation published
in the United States of America by:

RIZZOLI INTERNATIONAL PUBLICATIONS, INC.
712 Fifth Avenue/New York 10019

All rights reserved.
No parts of this book may be
reproduced in any manner whatsoever
without permission of
Rizzoli International Publications, Inc.

Translated from the French
by Howard Brabyn.

Library of Congress Catalog Card Number: 76-19193
ISBN: 0-8478-0062-8

Printed in France

Art

NE
674
D 394
J 3413

OUR world is a world without God, says André Malraux, that spokesman of our time. Yet never before has an anxious humanity set out so feverishly in quest of the supernal, following routes which, for the most part, are far removed from the traditional paths. Never before has the urge to seek after spirituality been so strong or so imbued with the sense of crisis. Never before have men embarked upon such a despairing pursuit of some eternal truth.

This search for God or the Supernatural, this need to transcend the ordinary, made manifest in countless irrational acts and gestures, is evidence of a mood of questioning and profound anguish.

If, however, as the confusion of the priesthood would seem to indicate, this world is a world without God, this does not mean that his existence is denied. Dogma may have been overturned, but the search for spirituality goes on as men grope for forms and havens in which it could remain alive. A new expression of faith is sought with an intensity unknown since the Reformation, because the forms that have served for centuries are now outworn. Our era is not an era of negation of the transcendental, but one of fundamental re-appraisal and questioning.

Artists, who mirror man's aspirations and foretell his hopes, reflect in their works, and indeed help to create, the visions of their time.

I spoke one day to Paul Delvaux about this dictum of Malraux. In his customary pensive manner the artist said, "Can one live without God?" By which he meant, "Can one create without God?" And at that moment the memory came back to me of Paulhan saying about Braque that "he painted in God." But is there not an element of the sacred in the painting of any great artist of our time? Is art possible without an element of the transcendental? To create is, precisely to "go beyond", to escape the realm of the real. Nothing that remains confined to the limits of reality can be considered art. Picasso spent his life constantly re-examining each verity the moment he felt he had arrived at one, rejecting it in order to continue the search for an absolute which, by this very fact, must necessarily be supernal.

All artists seek and test out, in silent solitude, the answers to this interrogation of an era in disarray. Solitude and silence—Delvaux's works are full of them. Perhaps this is why they evoke in us a feeling of unease. But this is not the only reason we feel disquiet. There is something else that moves us even more deeply; the essence of his work is drawn from the wellsprings of an art that once served the cause of the highest spirituality.

The question as to whether Delvaux's work is essentially sacred art deserves an in-depth study. In the limited space of this preface I shall confine myself to the broad outline of this hypothesis.

Rendering the invisible visible has, throughout the ages, been the secret basis of all creation, especially when applied to Christian beliefs in which the invisible, the ineffable was God. This can be seen in Romanesque art, that "foremost outpouring of the West" as Focillon called it, the most mysterious of western styles which summed up the dialogue between the everyday world and the world of faith. Whereas the Greek gods lost the divinity with which they were invested and were transformed into mere statues—we can no longer see them in any other way than Malraux does—Romanesque sculpture renders back to us the humble, burning faith that guided the hands of its anonymous creators. They carved the hours of the day, the passing of time, and still today we hear their voices singing out for Christendom to the glory of God. By what miracle did they manage to capture this feeling of sublime wonderment and transmit it across the centuries so that it continues to resound like the song of the universe? How is it that these stones, triumphing against time, have remained so many prayers? This ability to capture, living, the divine spirit, to present its eternal movement in visible form, remains one of the great mysteries of life for which no explanation is possible. As Braque said, "the only worthwhile things in art are those which cannot be explained." To grasp the invisible divine (leaving aside "religious iconography" which does not necessarily have this inner quality and, indeed, in presenting the outward form destroys this intangible aspect) and crystallize the invisible without turning it into mere stone in the process, to preserve the stirrings of the faith within tangible objects has been, it can be assumed, the artist's greatest dream.

The Gothic era, which followed an extraordinary period in which religion was all-powerful, passed on its message to Christendom in fulsome, still solemn tones, but also with tenderness. In France and in Flanders the invisible was still God and hymns were sung to his glory. Meanwhile, in the Italy of the *Quattrocento* religious fervour and the fascination of Giotto's art had given way, with Masaccio, Uccello and Piero della Francesca, to a heroic, humanistic spirituality. And this was a spirituality of quite another order to that of the Middle Ages for it was more than a question of a world of new art forms; here, particularly in painting, were manifest two different conceptions of man and his position vis-à-vis God. "Christian civilization," wrote Malraux, "until that moment a civilization of the soul, began its metamorphosis into a civilization of the spirit." But Gothic art is essentially romantic. Its exaltation and its tenderness belong to that current of romanticism which (like the classical current) flows through the whole of art quite independently of the movement which bears its name and which marked the beginning of the last century.

Phases of romanticism can be seen in all the great stylistic periods and one may ask whether this phase in the life of each great period was not precisely the point at which the search for the invisible took on a sacred character. Surrealism, the latest incarnation of romanticism of our era, rejected religion but affirmed the existence of the mystery of the world. The impetus, the feeling of communion, the wonder of the Gothic era, in short the very core of its art, created a climate of spirituality in which the Virgins of the altar screens were at one with those decorating the tympanum and the pages of the psalters.

The mannerists heightened the intensity and the hypnotic subtleties of eternal romanticism. In the people portrayed by Primatice and above all by Rosso, who seem to bring the medieval dream back to life, we recognize the ancestors of the figures who appear in Delvaux's paintings.

And now we can see the roots of Delvaux's art. His painting is not in the line of heroic humanism. It unfolds its vision in a somnambulistic ritual which draws on the wellsprings of Christianity. Despite the antique classical aspect of the forms portrayed, a point to which I shall return, Delvaux undoubtedly has links with the great romantics, those of the Sienna school and with Angelico rather than with Piero della Francesca. Delvaux's figures owe less to Olympus than to Chartres. They have the sovereign immobility, the sacerdotal splendour, the uprightness and the indifference to the world, even perhaps to life, of cathedral statues. Their solitude is complete. Their faces are lit up with a spirituality that flows from within and their shadowy gaze, untroubled by any emotion is that of statues. The ineffable shines through their tranquil features and their hands are poised almost in the gesture of blessing. "Never make your figures laugh or cry," advised the Rosicrucian Filiger, the spiritual heir of "those immortals Duccio and Cimabué."

Delvaux's art is not "powerful" art in the sense that that of Piero della Francesca, creator of the severe Tuscan style, is powerful. It is a tender art, and in its tenderness it is a return to the medieval vision which served God, not man. The woman who reigned over the world of Paul Delvaux is Eve rather than Venus. She is not unclothed, she is naked and therefore outside the realms of sensuality. Can one imagine a real life version of one of Delvaux's women? And this nakedness conjures up visions of the innocence of paradise before the Fall, rather than of Dionysian orgies, yet it conveys more than just the fact of nudity. This is not the human Greek nude of regal beauty, but the medieval nude, a graceful vision from a dream. We cannot stretch out our hands and touch Delvaux's nudes. They are symbols whose significance goes beyond what is portrayed, what is visible. Real yet inaccessible, recognizable yet mythical, these personages belong not to this world but to the magical world of poetry. Protagonists in some secret ceremony, motionless, with the air of having been struck by a lightning flash of revelation, they are participants in a rite at whose meaning we can guess but to which access is denied us.

This sense of holy fervour is imparted to us through the silence which reigns in Delvaux's works—silence, but also light and solitude. The seeming contradiction in Delvaux's works between the outward forms of the ancient world and the profound sense of the supernatural and the divine which they exude is more apparent than real. For Delvaux, the ancient pagan world is, as it were, his formal vocabulary, the chosen landscape against which his vision blossoms and his quest is placed. Throughout the ages, from the first Christians who cast the substance of their new faith in the mould of the Hellenistic inheritance, artists have drawn on the forms of the past against which they project their own visions.

For Delvaux, as for his spiritual predecessors, the ancient world is the chosen framework within which to reach out towards the invisible. The ancient world, but in particular Pompeii. Why Pompeii? Pompeii provides us with an occasion unique in the history of the world at which life as it was being lived—not merely an interpretation of life restored to us through art or any other means—was captured in full swing, in all its joy, and immobilized for eternity, an extraordinary moment at which death seized hold of life to transfix it for ever without reducing it to ashes and returning it to the void. This must be the sole example of death as the continuation of the form of life and not its negation. Seen in this way, the life-death encounter of Pompeii provides a crystallization of Delvaux's fascination for the encounter of strange elements that in the order of things are contradictory. The contradiction of this life-death encounter contains an element of the bizarre, the unusual which has never ceased to haunt the painter's imagination. "The sudden confrontation of drama and joy," was how he described the Spitzner museum. This preoccupation with the life-death motif can also be seen in the Crucifixion themes he tackled intermittently between 1943 and 1954, in which skeletons are portrayed adopting lifelike positions. Curiously, these pictures with religious themes are the ones which succeed the least in making the divine music ring out, perhaps because they are too anecdotal. The theme has risen to the surface of the picture and its externally religious tone seems to be the least imbued with spirituality. At Pompeii man's questioning about the mystery of the after-life is manifested in unexpected fashion, far removed from that to which religion has tried to furnish the answer. Here there is no other life, no heaven and no hell. Life has become form and this form envelops life which has no existence other than at the moment of being transfixed. For the artist anxious to penetrate the secret meaning of things and make it visible, this phenomenon so redolent of the mysteries of the world holds a special fascination. This questioning is closely linked to the faith which shows itself in Delvaux's visible forms expressed in terms of themes drawn from the world of outward appearances. It must be admitted that this has led to a widespread misunderstanding which has descended like a curtain between the artist's work and those who look at it. The latter take delight in it because they find it reassuring. They think they are looking at "a wordly spectacle," to use the artist's own terms whereas clearly the essence of these works resides in the "other-wordly spectacle" and this they sense and fear. These painting speak an intelligible language that anyone can decipher; everything in them is recognizable and the means of expression used are strictly classic. There are building that "look like" temples, perspective is respected, planes and volumes interlock in a coherent, plastic whole within the structure of each work. What then gives rise to this unease? Is it due merely to the fact that each one of these elements, natural as they are, seems to be related in unusual fashion to the other elements of the composition? This is not the only reason. The uneasiness one feels when looking at these paintings, after recognizing all the individual elements does not arise simply from the strange interrelationships the artist has given them. It arises from the fact that this inter-relationship also transfigures the reality of the individual elements. These temples, this perspective, these women are there not to affirm their reality but to produce a harmony in the musical sense of the term. These elements interact like the themes of a fugue and their harmony or disharmony brings out in us an emotion which stems from the realm of poetry. Suddenly we have the clear feeling that the essence of the work does not reside in the image it presents and we know that the riddle it sets us will not be solved and that the answer will escape us. The painter's language of form is derived from reality, from the banal. But is not all that is truly strange derived from banality and not from factitious concoctions or from the artificial which is the very opposite of the unusual?

Every creative artist has his roots in, and draws his references from, the visible world, nature, the nursery ground and leaven of all vision. But the apparent material reality of form is taken to such an extreme of intensity that it looks something quite other than itself. "All great figurative works resemble what they portray but it is the differences which make them works of art," said Malraux. Delvaux's recognizable elements are not reality portrayed in images. What separates him from reality, what becomes evident through the reality of his images, lit up as they are by a strange inner light, is his search for the transcendental which he can only achieve through the medium of poetry. He does not attempt to "illustrate" the transcendental, he creates it through the magic of poetry. His figures and his objects are deceptively familiar, for over and above their visible rhythm there lies the deeper mystery of the unfathomable which in the Far East is called "Invisible Reality" and in the Christian west "Truth."

How can the banal give rise to the supernatural except through the magic of poetry? How can we extract from "the apparent, the essence of that which does not belong to the realm of the apparent?" Here lies the secret of Delvaux's work and if we are to try to approach it we must do so in silence. We could not do better than to follow Jean Paulhan's advice on the best way to visit a church: "Approach it as you would a forest... don't attempt to go right across it all at once. Everyone has secrets of this kind for use in all aspects of life and everyone keeps his own secrets, without which he could not live..." We must not try to penetrate secrets all at once for they are an echo of the mysteries with which the world is filled. And Paulhan added: "the man who gives away his secrets is lost..." No doubt the smiles of Kores from the Acropolis would be less bewitching if we knew at what they were smiling. Delvaux's secret is stronger than his personages. His poetic force is stronger than his women and his work is impregnated with the stuff of dreams. His art lies in what cannot be seen, in that spirituality of which faith is the soul.

Thus we cannot enter Delvaux's universe. We are held at a distance. We hear the poetry and we feel the violence and the tenderness of his work in the very depths of our being. And these successive emotions, in Paulhan's fine phrase, bathe "our hands and our faces in the refreshing waters of a lost world."

*
* *

Someone asked Delvaux one day whether he made preparatory sketches for his engravings. "No," replied Delvaux, "because if I did there would be nothing left to discover..." This reply, which is rather similar to that of Braque when he said, "I find what I want where it finds me...," is doubly interesting: Firstly, because it is a confirmation of the considerable part that the unexpected plays in the creative act, and secondly, because it throws light on Delvaux's freedom of approach to his graphic work. This freedom is a combination of inspirational and inventive liberty and of availability to set to work immediately, though, of course, the technique has to be tamed and mastered if the inspiration is to shine through despite the constraints of a limited surface of a particular kind. "The one thing that interests me," Delvaux told me once, "is the risk I take each time I embark on a new work." This love of risk, of adventure, and therefore of danger, is the factor above all others that halts the sclerosis of ideas and prevents the wellspring of inspiration from coagulating and drying up. It explains Delvaux's youthful dash and sparkling freshness. How many times have I seen him bent over a lithographic stone or a sheet of transfer paper measuring his wits againts "the unexpected." And I recall the lines Jean Leymarie wrote recently about the composition of an illustrated book: "The virgin page of the book is like the face of dawn. In exalting each character and refining each line the word and the drawing we are seeking appear as if by magic on the page, just as the rising sun appears." No better description could be given of the artist before an untouched copper plate or lithographic stone.

How does Delvaux's silent poetry become embodied in the various techniques he uses, each with its own difficulties and its own special demands? In lithography, which he prefers to copper engraving—doubtless because of its greater ease of working and its flexibility which enables it more easily to accommodate sudden inspirational impulses—Delvaux remains essentially the painter. His light, his shade, his colour range remain close to that of his paintings. But his deep velvety blacks enhance the lightness of the background and stress the musical harmony of the drawing. The artist's wish is to efface the technique under the poetry of the theme so that the form "marries" the internal melody unconstrained by an over-obtrusive craftsmanship. "Nothing really exists except through poetry," says Jean Leymarie. The necessarily restricted surface of the stone or plate prevents the artist from developing the full richness of his theme as he can in his paintings. This constraint involves the artist in a sort of reduced scale of construction to which his creative urge finds it difficult to adapt. Hence his determination to treat these subjects as details of a painting, as key points cut out and isolated from an ideally much larger composition, just as in the cinema a close-up can bring out the essence of a monologue. This camera-like action, this spotlight trained on a single detail of a whole, capturing the image in the fixed stare of a single angle shot, gives it an intensity, a new dimension and accentuates the countless indications of what is to be seen outside the image we are shown. Around these heads of Pompeian women our imagination builds the villas and gardens of the deserted city bathed in the light of a summer's night. The shades of unending forests close round these women lost in silent reverie. All Delvaux's song is to be found condensed and compressed in his graphic work. This woman wearing a tiara-like headdress, with hands clasped at her breast, has the foreign flavour of a Byzantine icon. The engravings and lithographs capture the basic essence of the themes running through the artist's paintings distilling to greater purity the emotion we feel before these moving fragments which here find a new unity.

*
* *

This secret art which refuses to yield to us is yet strangely close to us because it reveals something about ourselves. It holds up a mirror to us in which we can but recognize ourselves. One of Pirandello's characters says: "I see flashes and lights, I have the impression of a glittering mirror... a mirror which must have gone mad..."

What is the affinity between the world of Delvaux and the world of Pirandello? The solitude which encloses Pirandello's characters, leaving them with nothing to contemplate save the enigma of their own lives, for which they are blameless, and which they seek desperately to unravel in the reflections it sends back to them, finds its echo in the work of Delvaux where unbroken silence reigns. "I have, at times," the artist said in an interview with Jacques Meuris, "depicted several women on a canvas, yet each of them was always alone..." The play of mirrors which is so important in Delvaux's work is just as important in Pirandello's world. "That buffoon that he failed to see in himself, but which he recognized in you who acted as his mirror..." The play of mirrors... The magic which in the illusory, deceptive aspect of what is apparent reveals the verity of the unfathomable. Magic also in its power to make us begin to imagine the nature of infinity.

*
* *

With its deep sense of solitude and its hallucinatory intensity, Delvaux's work is in a profound sense a work of our time. It acknowledges, by exalting it, the spiritual anguish of modern man and the disorder of a godless world seeking new foundations on which to build its hopes and dreams. In this Delvaux is truly a painter of *our* time, of the time we are living now; but yet his visionary grifts make him a painter of all the ages. His work is a multi-facetted mirror of the feelings and sentiments of an era, its dreams and its longings. Standing apart from all contemporary artistic trends, and with no dogmatic intent, it expresses the profound and pure values with which its poetry and universal dimension endow it. Lonely it is and free; and it is this poetic freedom which never ceases to move and astound us. Therein lies its secret power and its prophetic strength.

MIRA JACOB

The plates detailed in this book comprise a complete catalogue of the engravings and lithographs created by Paul Delvaux between 1966 and 1976.

The rare experimental works produced by the artist prior to this period are presented at the beginning of this book.

The cover and frontispiece are original lithographs created by Paul Delvaux specially for this book.

All the lithographs and etchings, with rare exceptions, were published by the *Galerie Le Bateau Lavoir*, Paris. This is not indicated, only the exceptions are noted.

Similarly, almost all the lithographs were printed by Fernand Mourlot and this is not indicated for each plate; only the rare cases where other printers were involved are noted.

In accordance with the usual practice, each print run includes a few artist's proofs, generally five to ten, as well as five to seven additional proofs reserved for those collaborating in their production and publication and for the deposition of duty copies. These extra proofs are not mentioned in the description of the prints.

The prints are usually signed in pencil by the artist. They are numbered in Arabic numerals, on the left, with the artist's signature on the right. An explanation is given for any other numerations used.

Dimensions are given in centimetres, first the height and then the width. The measurements of the format of each work are taken:
    for copperplate, from the edge of the dishing,
    for the lithographs from the edge of the subject matter.

The paper format measurements are those of the whole sheet of paper on which the work is printed.
The measurements of the subject matter formats are accurate, but the paper format measurements are only approximate and are given as an indication. This is because the paper used reacts unevenly under the press and may stretch to a greater or lesser degree. Thus the sheets may vary in size from four to eight millimetres, but never more than this.

If the date is to appear on the plate the right way round, the artist has to inscribe it on the stone in reverse. He does not always remember to do this which is why on some plates the dates appear reversed.

The abreviation S.H.W. often used in this book indicates the catalogue of paintings, compiled by Suzanne Houbart-Wilkin. Prefaces by Michel Butor and Jean Clair. Cosmos pub., Brussels 1975.

In 1960, Paul Delvaux was an art teacher at the *Ecole des Arts Plastiques de la Cambre.* He had never tried his hand at copperplate engraving but one day, while visiting an engraving workshop with his pupils, he decided he would like to experiment and he engraved a half-length portrait of a woman on a small plate (No. 1).

Fascinated by the technique, he made two variants on this theme (Nos. 2 and 3) and later the same year he did a larger etching, *Tender Night* (No. 4).

But these were only experiments made for his own pleasure and he did not persevere with them.

It was not until 1966 that he resumed his experiments and his exploration of the rich field of engraving and lithography which was to become a passion with him.

1960

Black and white etching
Subject format: 14.7 × 11.3 cm
Paper format: 25 × 22 cm

This was Paul Delvaux's very first attempt at this technique. The plate and one or two trial proofs were kept by the artist.
No print run was made in 1960.
In 1967, 100 signed and numbered proofs were run off on Arches paper and were inserted in the first 100 copies of Paul Aloïse de Bock's book *Paul Delvaux*, Laconti pub. Brussels, 1967.

Ref. No. 45 of *Cahier Paul Delvaux No. 3*, Le Bateau Lavoir, publisher (B.L. pub.), Paris, 1972.

2. HALF-LENGTH PORTRAIT OF A WOMAN II

1960

Etching
Second version of the previous subject (No. 1)

Subject format: 14.7 × 11.3 cm
Arches paper format: 32.5 × 25.5 cm
Japan paper format: 32.5 × 25.5 cm

Signature on the copperplate at bottom right: P. Delvaux
The initials P.D. appear underneath. Undated.

The copperplate and one or two trial proofs made in 1960 were kept by the
artist. No print run was made in 1960. 70 proofs were run off in 1971:
50 black and white proofs on Arches paper, signed and numbered.
20 proofs in sanguine on Japan paper, signed and numbered in Roman
numerals. Printer Leblanc, Paris. Plate defaced.

Ref. No. 46 of *Cahier Paul Delvaux No. 3*, B.L. pub., Paris, 1972.

1960

Alternative title:
THE BOOK

Black and white etching

Subject format: 14.7 × 11.3 cm
Paper format: 26.5 × 19 cm

This third version of the same subject was the only one of which a series of prints was made in 1960.

It was originally intended to include this etching in a book of engravings by surrealist artists. However, the book was never published.
60 signed and numbered proofs on Rives paper. The numbering and signature are unusual in that they are done in ink and are both on the same side, the right. Schwartz pub., Milan. The plate has been preserved.

Ref. No. 47 of *Cahier Paul Delvaux No. 3*, B.L. pub., Paris, 1972.

4. TENDER NIGHT

1960

Black and white etching

Subject format: 29.5 × 19.2 cm
Arches paper format: 49.5 × 32.5 cm
Japan paper format: 51 × 33.5 cm

The plate and a few trial proofs made in 1960 were kept by the artist.

65 proofs were run off in 1969:

50 proofs on Arches paper, signed and numbered.
15 proofs on Japan paper, signed and numbered in Roman numerals.
Printer Lacourière, Paris.

Plate defaced.

Reproduced in the book *Les Dessins de Paul Delvaux*, preface by Maurice Nadeau, Denoël, Paris and Propyläen, Berlin pub. 1967, page 82.

Two years later the artist painted two canvases based on the same theme—*Les Demoiselles de Tongres*, 1962, S.H.W. No. 266, and *Tender Night*, 1962, reproduced in S.H.W. No. 268.

Ref. No. 48 of *Cahier Paul Delvaux No. 3*, B.L. pub., Paris, 1972.

4. TENDER NIGHT

Paul Delvaux's début in the field of engraving and lithography occurred towards the end of 1965. Some fine drawing on transfer paper, in lithographic crayon, were transferred to stone by Mourlot with his usual meticulous care. This operation was achieved to the artist's satisfaction and, in early 1966, Paul Delvaux's first four lithographs saw the light of day.

The Rivals, *January 1966*
The Two Friends, *January 1966*
Anne Lost in Thought, *February 1966*
The Sea is Near, *February 1966*

For *The Rivals* and *Anne Lost in Thought* the artist superimposed colours on the black and white drawing, a practice which he often followed later.

Delvaux wanted to leave *The Two Friends* in the black and white state and it was decided to print a limited run of 15 proofs.

Since *The Sea is Near* had not been transferred to stone to his entire satisfaction, Delvaux decided to make some alterations directly on the stone. This he did when he returned to Paris for the first time after a long absence.

5. THE RIVALS

January 1966

Colour lithograph

The theme of this lithograph, the first created by Paul Delvaux, is one of that is dear to the artist—the strange silence of beings who, all unseeing, pass by each other.

Subject format: 65 × 50.5 cm. Paper format: 76.5 × 56.5 cm.

The black state was drawn in lithographic crayon on transfer paper and transferred to stone. Zincs were used for the colours. A few trial proofs of the black only.

In the first state the plate bore the following four-line inscription: Les Rivales / Boitsfort / P. Delvaux / 1-66. Of this state: 2 trial proofs.

For the final printing the artist erased the first three lines of the inscription, leaving only the date: 1-66.

75 signed and numbered proofs on Arches paper.
Stone polished out.

Reproduced in colour in *Les Dessins de Paul Delvaux*, preface by Maurice Nadeau, Denoël, Paris and Propyläen, Berlin pub. 1967, page 97.

The theme of this plate should be compared with that of the artist's *Breakwater*, produced in the same year (1966) reproduced in *Paul Delvaux* by Paul-A. de Bock, Laconti pub., Brussels, and J.-J. Pauvert, pub., Paris, 1967, No. 165, page 243, and in S.H.W. No. 297.

There is also a large water-colour, preliminary to the lithograph, which bears the same title *The Rivals*. Reproduced in *Les Dessins de Paul Delvaux*, Denoël, Paris and Propyläen, Berlin pub. 1967, page 103.

Ref. No. 2 of *Cahier Paul Delvaux No. 1*, B.L. pub., Paris, 1966.

5. THE RIVALS

6. THE TWO FRIENDS

January 1966

Lithograph in black

One state only
Subject format: 65.5 × 50.5 cm
Paper format: 76.5 × 56.5 cm

Dated on the stone, bottom right: 1-66
Lithographic crayon on transfer paper transferred to stone

15 signed and numbered proofs on Arches paper.
5 proofs touched up by the artist, by hand in Indian ink and water-colours, signed and numbered in Roman numerals.
Stone polished out.

Reproduced in *Les Dessins de Paul Delvaux*, Denoël, Paris and Propyläen, Berlin pub. 1967, page 83.

Ref. No. 12 of *Cahier Paul Delvaux No. 2*, B.L. pub., Paris, 1969.
(In the *Cahier* the format width is erroneously given as 51.5 cm).

7. ANNE LOST IN THOUGHT

February 1966

Colour lithograph

Subject format: 65 × 51 cm
Paper format: 76 × 56.5 cm

Signature and date on the stone, bottom right: P. Delvaux 2-66

Drawing in crayon on lithographic paper, transferred to stone for the background. Zincs were used for the colours. Some trial proofs were made of the black state only.

75 signed and numbered proofs on Arches paper.

Stone polished out.

Reproduced in *Les Dessins de Paul Delvaux*, Denoël, Paris and Propyläen, Berlin pub. 1967, page 95.

Ref. No. 1 of *Cahier Paul Delvaux No. 1*, B.L. pub., Paris, 1966.

8. THE SEA IS NEAR

February 1966

Lithograph in black

Subject format: 64.5 × 50.5 cm
Paper format: 76 × 56.5 cm

Dated on the stone, bottom right: 2-66

Lithographic crayon on transfer paper, transferred to stone
Considerable touching up on the actual stone

One state only

75 signed and numbered proofs
Stone polished out

Reproduced in *Les Dessins de Paul Delvaux*, Denoël, Paris and Propyläen, Berlin pub. 1967, page 99.

The theme of this lithograph should be compared with that of the painting of the same name, *The Sea is Near*, 1965, reproduced in Paul-A. de Bock's *Paul Delvaux*, Laconti pub., Brussels 1967, and J.-J. Pauvert, pub., Paris, plate 163, page 240, and in S.H.W. No. 295.

There is also a large wash drawing with the same title, reproduced in *Les Dessins de Paul Delvaux*, Denoël, Paris and Propyläen, Berlin pub., 1967, page 93, and in *Cahier Paul Delvaux No. 1*, B.L. pub., 1966, No. 10.

Ref. No. 13 of *Cahier Paul Delvaux No. 2*, B.L. pub., Paris, 1969.

8. THE SEA IS NEAR

His interest and curiosity aroused by his early experiments with lithography, Paul Delvaux was anxious to explore more fully the possibilities offered by this technique.

He decided to come to Paris. His links with the capital, broken twenty years earlier, were renewed in almost miraculous fashion, thanks mainly to a group of men whose craftsmanship, warmth and communicativeness made of them a unique team — the staff of the Mourlot workshop. Adopted by them immediately on a basis of respect and friendship, he felt happy and unconstrained in working with and among them.

He produced his first lithograph drawn directly on stone. The finesse and the subtlety of line afforded by this technique and the opportunities it provided for the modulation of light and shade — basic constants of his art — captivated the artist who set to work with intense pleasure.

Realizing the new vistas and new discoveries that this technique, so closely allied to drawing yet so individual and one which allowed him to "paint" on the stone itself, could offer him, be became passionately attached to lithography.

During subsequent years he stayed often and regularly in Paris.

This was the commencement of a series of works on stone which produced a number of plates which count among the finest in lithographic art.

9. THE SECRET

March 1966

Lithograph in black

Subject format: 65 × 50 cm
Paper format: 76 × 56.5 cm

Date is reversed on the stone, bottom left: 30-3-66
Lithographic crayon on stone
One state only

75 signed and numbered proofs on Arches paper

Stone polished out

Ref. No. 4 of *Cahier Paul Delvaux No. 1*, B.L. pub., Paris, 1972.

10. MIRRORS

June 1966

Lithograph in black.

Subject format: 50 × 66 cm.
Paper format: 56.5 × 76.5 cm

Date on the stone, bottom right:
6-66.
Lithographic ink, pen and wash drawing
on stone.

One state only.

50 signed and numbered proofs
on Arches paper.
10 signed proofs on Arches paper,
numbered in Roman numerals,
and touched up by hand in water
colour by the artist.

Stone polished out.

Reproduced in *Les Dessins
de Paul Delvaux*, Denoël, Paris and
Propyläen, Berlin pub. 1967,
page 70.

Ref. No. 3 of *Cahier Paul Delvaux No. 1*,
B.L. pub., Paris, 1966.

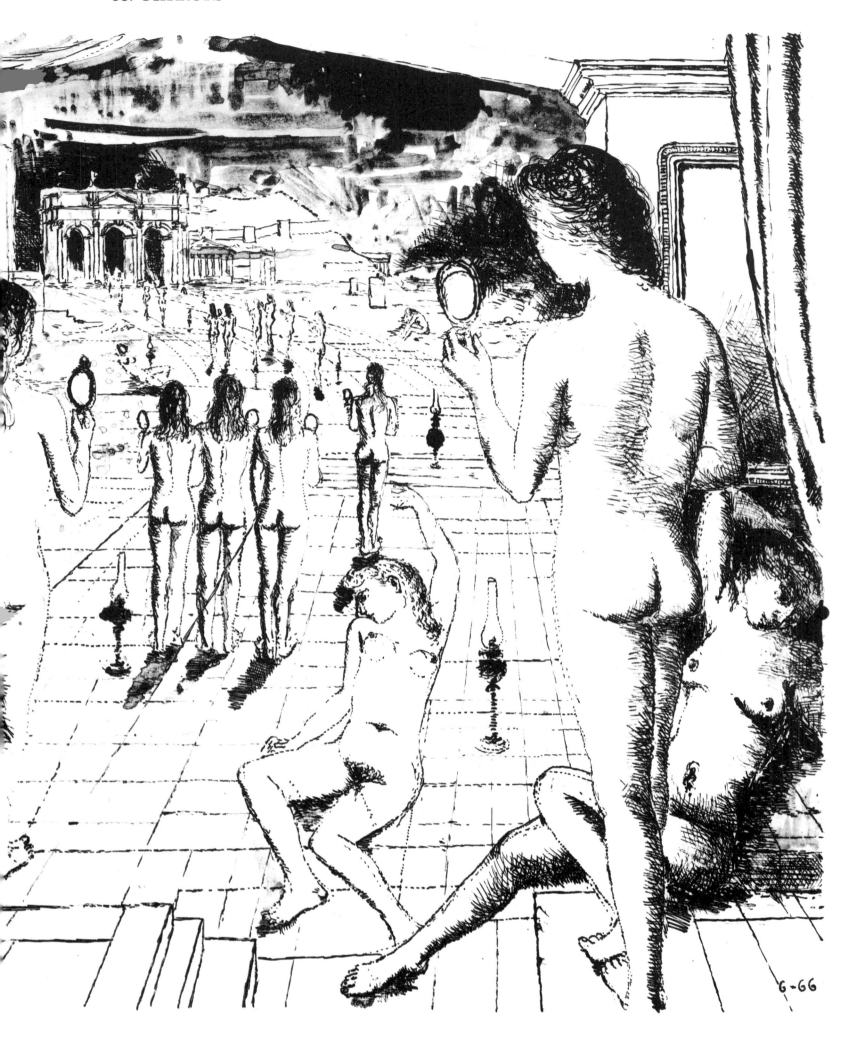

G-66

October 1966

Lithograph in black
Lithographic crayon on stone

No. 11: 1st state. The subject is smaller than in the final state and has an encircling line. Format 24 × 19.5 cm. The date is inscribed on the stone, bottom right: 10·66. 2 trials proofs.

No. 12: Final state. The artist has removed the line encircling the composition which he has enlarged on all four sides.
In the final state can be seen traces of the original limits of the composition and its enlargement beyond the removed line. The date has been eliminated.

Formats: subject 31.5 × 25 cm, paper 65.5 × 50.5 cm.

65 signed and numbered proofs on Arches paper.

Ref. No. 19 of *Cahier Paul Delvaux No. 2*, B.L. pub., Paris, 1969.

12. LADY WITH THE CANDLE

This lithograph was used as the poster and the cover of the catalogue puhished on the occasion of the exhibition of the artist's first lithographs *(Cahier Paul Delvaux No. 1)* at the gallery *Le Bateau Lavoir*, in November 1966.

250 copies of the original poster, on an ochre background, were made.
The central part of the composition, 20.2 × 25 cm, was used for the catalogue cover. Total width of the cover: 20.2 × 60 cm. 1,000 copies of the catalogue were printed.
Stone polished out.

13. YOUNG GIRLS

March 1967

Lithograph in black
Subject format: 65.5 × 49.5 cm
Paper format: 76.5 × 56.5 cm

Lithographic ink, wash drawing, pen and brush on stone
Date on the stone, bottom right: 1-3-67
One state only
75 signed and numbered proofs on Arches paper
Stone polished out

Ref. No. 16 of *Cahier Paul Delvaux No. 2*, B.L. pub., Paris, 1969

14. THREE WOMEN

February 1967

Lithograph in black
Subject format: 53.5 × 74.5 cm
Arches paper format: 58 × 79 cm
Old buff paper format: 62 × 82.5 cm
Lithographic ink, wash drawing, pen and brush on stone
Several scrapings
Date on the stone, bottom right: 28-2-67
One state only

50 signed and numbered proofs on Arches paper
10 *hors commerce* (not for sale) signed proofs on old buff paper,
marked H.C. 1 to H.C. 10
Stone polished out

This lithograph could well have been entitled *Homage to Picasso*. Paul Delvaux drew it after visiting the final day of an exhibition at the *Bibliothèque Nationale* devoted to Picasso's lithographs and engravings (November 1966 to February 1967). Delvaux was profoundly impressed by the Spanish artist's work.

Reproduced in *Les Dessins de Paul Delvaux*, Denoël, Paris and Propyläen, Berlin pub. 1967, page 112.

Ref. No. 14 of *Cahier Paul Delvaux No. 2*, B.L. pub., Paris, 1969. ➡

28-2-67

15. MAUVE CURTAINS

November 1967

Colour lithograph on stone

Subject format: 36.2 × 27 cm
Paper format 37.7 × 28 cm

100 signed and numbered proofs on Lana laid paper.
30 *hors commerce* (not for sale) proofs on Lana laid paper, signed and numbered in Roman numerals, H.C. I to H.C. XXX.
A few trial proofs of the black only.

These proofs were inserted in the first 130 copies of the book *Les Dessins de Paul Delvaux*, preface by Maurice Nadeau, Denoël, Paris pub. 1967.

Format of the book 40 × 30 cm.

Kayser printer, Brussels.

Ref. No. 49 of *Cahier Paul Delvaux No. 3*, B.L. pub., Paris, 1972.

15. MAUVE CURTAINS

2-3-67.

16. WOMAN'S FACES

March 1967

Lithograph in black

Subject format: 40 × 30 cm. Paper format: 53 × 38 cm

Drawing in lithographic ink, pen and brush on stone.
Date on the stone, bottom right: 2-3-67.
One state only.

65 signed and numbered proofs on Arches paper.

Stone polished out.

A portion of this lithograph, format 20 × 30 cm, was used for the cover of *Cahier Paul Delvaux No. 2*, published for the exhibition "Paul Delvaux dessins et lithographies 1966-1969", at the gallery *Le Bateau Lavoir*, Paris May 1969. 1,500 copies of the Cahier were made.
Ref. No. 17 of *Cahier Paul Delvaux No. 2*, B.L. pub., Paris, 1969.

17 and 18. SUNDAY DRESS

June 1967

Lithograph in two states
Date on the stone, bottom right: 6-6-67

No. 17: Black state.
Subject format: 63.5 × 51 cm. Paper format: 76 × 55.5 cm

Lithographic crayon on stone

50 signed and numbered proofs on Arches paper

Reproduced in *Les Dessins de Paul Delvaux*, Denoël, Paris and Propyläen, Berlin pub. 1967, page 108.

No. 18: Colour state.
Subject format: 63.5 × 51 cm. Paper format: 76 × 56 cm
For this state the artist used the black of the previous plate on which he superimposed colours. Colours on zincs.

75 signed and numbered proofs on Arches paper.
Stone polished out

There is also a preliminary water colour dated 1-6-67, reproduced in *Cahier Paul Delvaux No. 2*, B.L. pub., Paris 1969, plate No. 25.

Ref. No. 15 of *Cahier Paul Delvaux No. 2*, B.L. pub., Paris, 1969. ➡

17. SUNDAY DRESS

6 · 6 · 67

18. SUNDAY DRESS

6-6-67

19. THE VISIT

1968

Etching in black
One state only

Subject format: 39.5 × 28 cm
Auvergne paper format: 56.5 × 38 cm
Japan Hodumura format: 50 × 36 cm

30 signed and numbered proofs on Auvergne parchment from the Richard de Bas paper-mill.
20 proofs on Japan Hodomura paper, signed and numbered in Roman numerals.

Printer Lacourière, Paris

Copper plate defaced

Ref. No. 23 of *Cahier Paul Delvaux No. 2*, B.L. pub., Paris, 1969.

March 1968
Lithograph in two states. Date on the stone, bottom right: 3-68
Black state: subject format: 63.5 × 47.5 cm, paper format: 76 × 56.5 cm
Lithographic crayon on stone. 75 signed and numbered proofs on Arches paper

March 1968

Colour state: subject format: 64.5 × 47.5 cm, paper format: 76 × 56.5 cm. This colour plate
is based on the preceding black plate. Colour on zincs. 2 trials proofs without the blue. 75 signed
and numbered proofs on Arches paper. Stone polished out.
Ref. No. 20 of *Cahier Paul Delvaux No. 2*, B.L. pub., Paris, 1969.

22 and 23. THE ENDS OF THE EARTH

December 1968

Lithograph in two states
Date on the stone, bottom right: 12-68

No. 22: Black state.

Subject format: 52 × 74.5 cm
Paper format: 65 × 85 cm.

Lithographic ink, pen and brush on stone
50 signed and numbered proofs on Arches paper

No. 23: Colour state.

Subject format: 52 × 75 cm
Paper format: 65 × 86 cm

The previous lithograph in black was used as the background of this colour composition.
Each of the colours was transferred to zinc and then printed on the background of the black and white drawing.

75 signed and numbered proofs on Arches paper.
Stone polished out.

The theme of this lithograph was also to be that of a painting bearing the same title, *The Ends of the Earth*, 1969, reproduced in S.H.W. No. 310. *Rétrospective Paul Delvaux* at the *Musée des Arts Décoratifs*, 1969, No. 74 in the catalogue.

Ref. No. 18 of *Cahier Paul Delvaux No. 2*, B.L. pub., Paris, 1969.

22. THE ENDS OF THE EARTH

Nº 23 ➡

24. EVE

February 1968

Etching in two states. Date on the copper plate, bottom right: 2-68
Formats: subject 39.5 × 27.5 cm; Auvergne paper 57 × 38.5 cm;
Japan Hodomura paper: 36 × 50.5 cm
Black state. 20 proofs: 10 on Japan Hodomura paper and 10 on Auvergne parchment,
signed and numbered in Roman numerals. Proofs I/XX to X/XX on Japan Hodomura. Proofs XI/XX to XX/XX on Auvergne parchment from the Richard de Bas
paper-mill.

25. EVE

February 1968

Colour state
Subject format: 39.5 × 27.5 cm. Paper format: 54 × 37.5 cm
30 signed and numbered proofs on Rives B.F.K.
Printer Lacourière, Paris
Copper plate defaced

Ref. No. 21 of *Cahier Paul Delvaux No. 2*, B.L. pub., Paris, 1969.

26. STAINED-GLASS WINDOW

June 1969

Etching printed in black

Subject format: 39.4 × 27.3 cm
Rives paper format: 65 × 50 cm
Japan Hodomura paper format: 63 × 47 cm

Date on the copper plate, bottom right: 6-69
One state only

50 signed and numbered proofs on Rives paper.
20 proofs *hors commerce* (not for sale) on Japan Hodomura, signed and numbered H.C. I to H.C. XX.
10 proofs on Rives paper touched up by hand in water colour by the artist, signed and numbered I/X to X/X.

These proofs, with the exceptions of those touched up, were inserted in the first copies of *Cahier de l'Herne*, issue of October 1974, devoted to Jules Verne.

Printer Lacourière, Paris.
Copper plate defaced.

Ref. No. 36 of *Cahier Paul Delvaux No. 3*, B.L., Paris, 1972.

27. THE QUARREL

June 1969

Etching printed in black

Subject format: 38.3 × 51.5 cm
Rives paper format: 56 × 72.5 cm
Japan Imperial paper format: 50.5 × 72 cm
Japan Kozu paper format: 61 × 80 cm
(Two different types of Japan paper with different dimensions were used.
Both dimensions are therefore given here.)
Rice paper format: 54 × 65.5 cm
Date on the copper plate, bottom right: 6-69
One state only

50 signed and numbered proofs on Rives paper
10 proofs on old Japan paper and rice paper, signed and numbered in Roman numerals.
Proofs I/X to V/X on different Japan papers
Proofs VI/X to X/X on rice paper

Printer Lacourière, Paris
Copper plate defaced

Réf. No. 31 of *Cahier Paul Delvaux No. 3,* B.L. pub., Paris, 1972. ➡

28. THE SIREN

September 1969

Colour lithograph
Subject format: 31 × 23.5 cm
Paper format: 32.5 × 25 cm

Date on the stone, reversed, bottom left: 9-69

Lithographic crayon on transfer paper, transferred to stone. Zincs for the colours. No proofs were made of the black state.

150 signed and numbered proofs for the deluxe copies of Gerhard Hauptmann's book *Das Meerwunder*, which also includes 4 reproductions of wash drawings by the artist. Propyläen pub., Berlin 1970. Format of the book: 35 × 28 cm. A few trial proofs of the black only.
A few wide-margined artist's proofs.
Stone polished out.

Ref. No. 50 of *Cahier Paul Delvaux No. 3*, B.L. pub., Paris, 1972.

29. THE ROOM

June 1969

Etching printed in black.

Subject format: 38.5 × 51 cm
Auvergne paper format:
58.5 × 79.5 cm
Format of various Japan papers:
51 × 72 cm
and 51 × 67 cm.

Date on the plate,
bottom right: 6-69.
One state only.

50 signed and numbered proofs
on Auvergne parchment
from the Richard de Bas paper-mill.
10 proofs on various Japan papers,
signed and numbered
in Roman numerals.

Printer Lacourière, Paris.
Copper plate defaced.

Ref. No. 33 of *Cahier Paul Delvaux No. 3*,
B.L. pub., Paris, 1972.

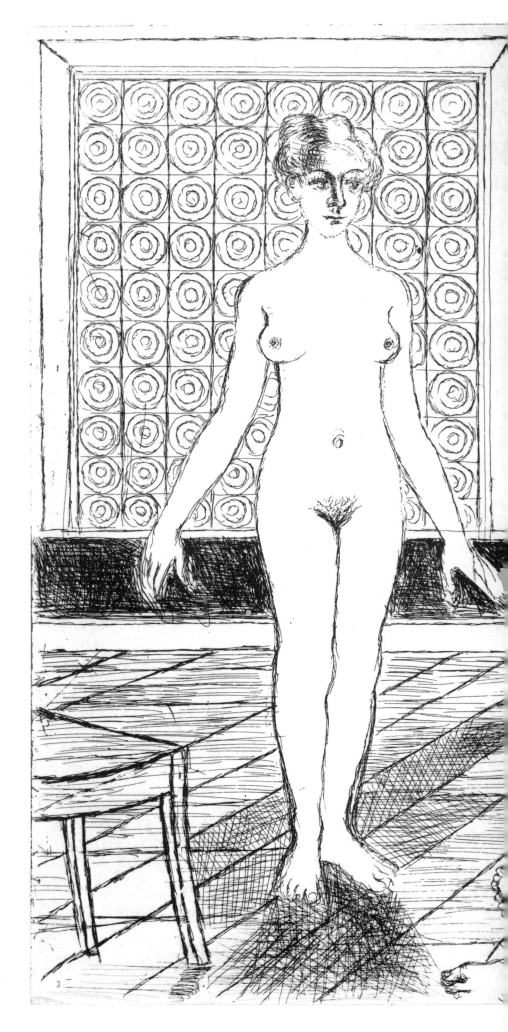

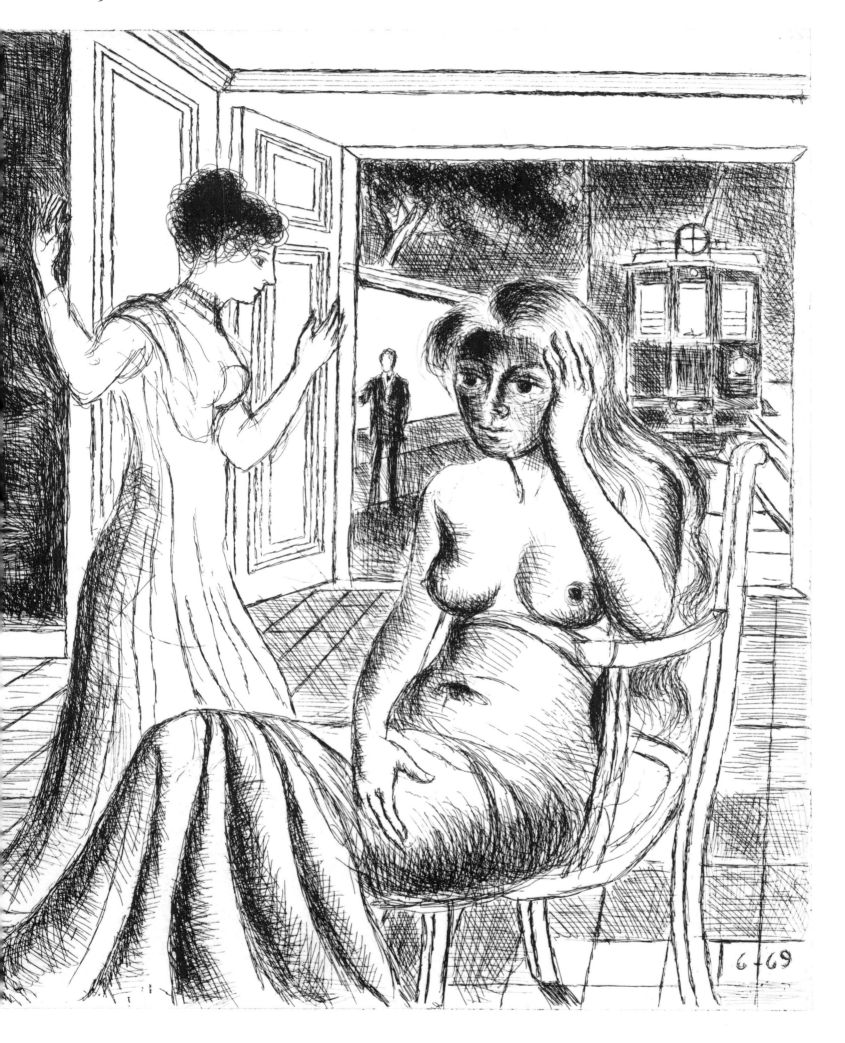

6-69

30. PROMÉTHÉE

October 1969

Lithograph in black
Subject format: 31 × 23.5 cm
Paper format: 45.5 × 36 cm

Crayon on lithographic paper transferred to stone.
Date on the stone, bottom left: 10-69
One state only

30 signed and numbered proofs on Arches paper
5 *hors commerce* (not for sale) proofs, signed and numbered in Roman numerals
H.C. I to H.C. V

Stone polished out

Ref. No. 27 of *Cahier Paul Delvaux No. 3*, B.L. pub., Paris, 1972

31. BLUE AZALEA

October 1969

Lithograph in two states   Black state.

Formats: subject 30.5 × 23.5 cm; paper 45.5 × 36 cm. Date, reversed, on the stone, bottom left: 10-69. Lithographic crayon on transfer paper, transferred to stone for the black. Zincs for the colours. 75 signed and numbered proofs on Arches paper.

October 1969

Colour state: same formats as the black state
75 signed and numbered proofs on Arches paper
Stone polished out
Ref. No. 32 of *Cahier Paul Delvaux No. 3*, B.L. pub., Paris, 1972

33. BY THE TOWN

November 1969

Lithograph in black.

Subject format: 48 × 65.5 cm
Paper format: 57 × 76 cm

Lithographic crayon on stone.
Date on the stone, bottom right:
11-69.
One state only.

75 signed and numbered
proofs on Arches paper.
Stone polished out.

This theme was taken up
by the artist for the painting
Nightfall, 1970,
reproduced in S.H.W. No. 315,
and for a large water-colour.

Ref. No. 29 of *Cahier Paul Delvaux No. 3*,
B.L. pub., Paris, 1972.

34. HAT WITH FLOWERS

June 1969

Lithograph in three states

Subject format: 31.5 × 23.5 cm
Paper format: 45.5 × 36 cm

Date, reversed, on the stone, bottom left: 6-69

No. 34: Black state.
Crayon on lithographic paper, transferred to stone
50 signed and numbered proofs on Arches paper
This plate served as the basis of two colour lithographs

35. HAT WITH FLOWERS I

June 1969

1st colour state
Subject format: 31.5 × 23.5 cm
Paper format: 45.5 × 36 cm

The artist added colours on zincs to the black plate (No. 34)
75 signed and numbered proofs on Arches paper

36. HAT WITH FLOWERS II

June 1969

2nd colour state
Subject format: 31.5 × 23.5 cm
Paper format: 45.5 × 36 cm
The artist revised the previous plate, modifying the colours
and adding four new ones, thus creating the third version of this composition

75 signed and numbered proofs on Arches paper
Stone polished out

Ref. No. 28, 28A and 28B of *Cahier Paul Delvaux No. 3*, B.L. pub., Paris, 1972

November 1969

Lithograph in two states   Black state.

Formats: subject 30.5 × 23.5 cm; paper 45.5 × 36 cm

Date, reversed, on the stone, bottom left: 11-69. Lithographic crayon on transfer paper,
transferred to stone for the black. Zincs for the colours.

75 signed and numbered proofs on Arches paper.

38. THE DANCE

November 1969

Colour state: same formats as the black state
75 signed and numbered proofs on Arches paper
Stone polished out
Ref. No. 30 of *Cahier Paul Delvaux No. 3*, B.L. pub., Paris, 1972.

39. PHRYNÉ

November 1969

Lithograph in two states   Black state.

Formats: subject 30.7 × 23.5 cm; paper 45.5 × 36 cm

Date, reversed on the stone, bottom left: 11-69. Lithographic crayon on transfer paper, transferred to stone for the black. Zincs for the colours.

75 signed and numbered proofs on Arches paper

40. PHRYNÉ

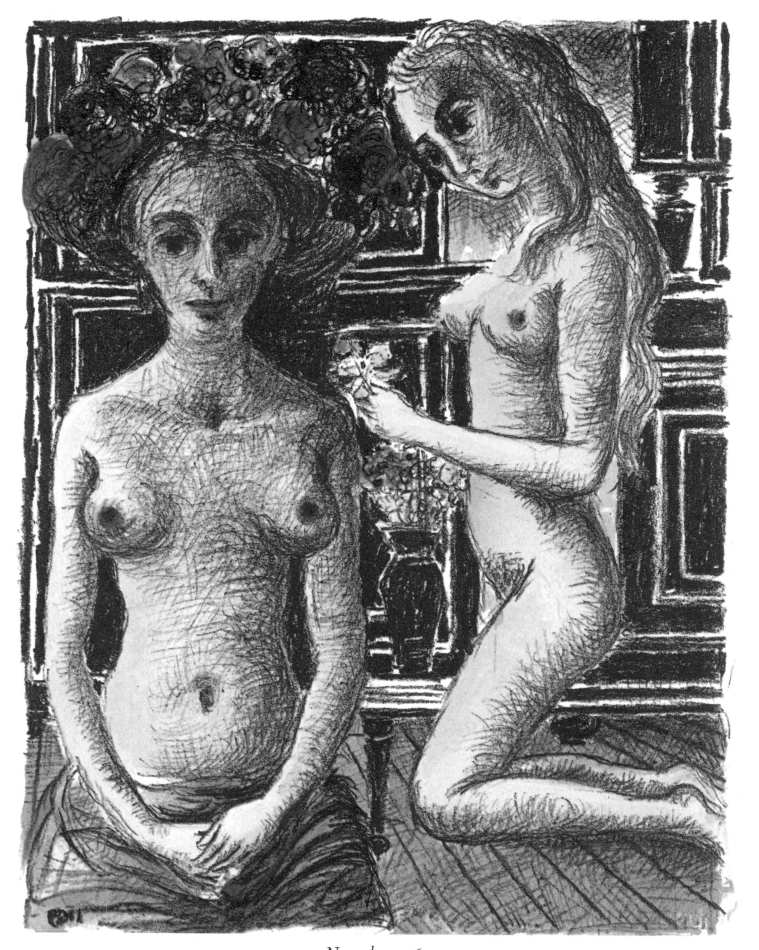

November 1969

Colour state: same formats as the black state
75 signed and numbered proofs on Arches paper
Stone polished out
Ref. No. 34 of *Cahier Paul Delvaux No. 3*, B.L. pub., Paris, 1972.

1-70

41. POMPEIAN WOMEN

January 1970

Lithograph in black
Subject format: 41.3 × 30.5 cm
Paper format: 65 × 50.5 cm

One state only
Lithographic crayon on stone
Date on the stone, bottom right: 1-70

50 signed and numbered proofs on Arches paper
Stone polished out

Ref. No. 38 of *Cahier Paul Delvaux No. 3*, B.L. pub., Paris, 1972

42. LOCOMOBILE

June 1970

Lithograph in black
Subject format: 60 × 80 cm
Paper format: 73.5 × 105 cm

One state only
Lithographic crayon on transfer paper, transferred to stone
Date, reversed, on the stone, bottom left: 6-70

3 trial proofs printed in bistre
75 signed and numbered proofs on Arches paper
Stone polished out

Ref. No. 35 of *Cahier Paul Delvaux No. 3*, B.L. pub., Paris, 1972. ➡

43. THE FOREST

June 1971

Lithograph in black
Subject format: 41 × 30 cm
Arches paper format: 60.5 × 42.5 cm
Japan paper format: 61 × 42 cm

One state only.
Lithographic ink on zinc.
Date reversed on the plate, bottom left: 6-71.

50 signed and numbered proofs on Arches paper.
25 proofs on Japan paper, signed and numbered in Roman numerals.

This lithograph was created in 1971 and signed in 1973. It was used as a poster for the exhibition "Paul Delvaux, graphic work, 1966-1973", at the Östergard Gallery at Svalöv, Sweden, 1973.
500 copies of the poster with text were printed.
Zinc polished out.

Ref. No. 33 of the catalogue *Paul Delvaux, graphic work*, Östergard Gallery, Svalöv, Sweden, 1973.

44 and 45. SLEEP

October 1970

Lithograph in two states

Subject format: 46 × 65 cm
Paper format: 62 × 90 cm

Date, reversed, on the stone, bottom left: 10-70

No. 44: Black state.

Lithographic crayon on transfer paper, transferred to stone.

50 signed and numbered proofs on Arches paper.

No. 45: Colour state.

The plate of the previous black state was used again by the artist as the background of this colour composition. Each of the colours was transferred to zinc and superimposed on the black state.

75 signed and numbered proofs on Arches paper
Stone polished out

Ref. No. 37 of *Cahier Paul Delvaux No. 3*, B.L. pub., Paris, 1972.

44. SLEEP

N° 45 ➡

05-01

June 1971

Lithograph. Formats: subject 31 × 24 cm; Arches paper 58 × 47 cm; Japan paper 58.5 × 47 cm
Date on the stone, bottom right: 6-71. Lithographic crayon on transfer paper, transferred to stone.
75 signed and numbered proofs on Arches paper, printed in black.   25 proofs on Japan paper,
printed in sanguine, signed and numbered in Roman numerals.   Stone polished out
Ref. No. 40 of *Cahier Paul Delvaux No. 3*, B.L. pub., Paris 1972

January 1971

Lithograph in two states

Subject format: 56 × 76 cm
Paper format: 66.5 × 90 cm

Date, reversed, on the stone, bottom left: 1-71

No. 47: Black state.
     Lithographic crayon on transfer paper, transferred to stone.
     50 signed and numbered proofs on Arches paper.

No. 48: Colour state.
The plate of the previous black state was used again by the artist as the background of this colour composition.
Each of the colours was transferred to zinc and superimposed on the black state.
75 signed and numbered proofs on Arches paper. Stone polished out.
This theme was to be used again by the artist in July 1971 for his painting *The Garden*; reproduced in S.H.W., No. 319, and on the cover of the catalogue for the great *Paul Delvaux* retrospective exhibition at the Tokyo and Kyoto Museums in 1975.

Ref. No. 42 of *Cahier Paul Delvaux No. 3*, B.L. pub., 1972.

→

49. ANNE, FULL FACE

June 1971

Lithograph

Subject format: 31 × 24 cm
Arches paper format: 58 × 48.5 cm
Japan paper format: 58 × 47 cm

Date on the stone, bottom right: 6-71
Crayon on lithographic paper, transferred to stone

75 signed and numbered proofs printed in black on Arches paper
25 proofs printed in sanguine on Japan paper, signed and numbered in Roman numerals
Stone polished out

Ref. No. 41 of *Cahier Paul Delvaux No. 3*, B.L. pub., Paris, 1972

50. THE LOVER

February 1971

Lithograph in two states
Subject format: 50 × 66 cm
Arches paper format: 58 × 76.5 cm
Japan paper format: 55 × 77 cm

Lithographic ink on stone
One state only
Date on the stone, bottom right: 17-2-71

Printed in black on a grey tinted background for the proofs on Arches paper,
without the grey tinted background for the proofs on Japan paper

75 signed and numbered proofs on Arches paper
25 proofs on Japan paper, signed and numbered in Roman numerals

The sharpness and incisiveness of this pen-drawn lithograph give it the appearance of an etching. It is, nevertheless, a pure lithograph. Stone polished out.

Ref. No. 39 of *Cahier Paul Delvaux No. 3*, B.L. pub., Paris, 1972 ➡

17-2-71

"This obscure world which must be expressed in the most ordinary terms... Not the externalities, but the breath, the essence of life..."
Jacques Rivière

The train forms one of the major themes of Paul Delvaux's work. In The Fabulous Journey, *the composition with the prophetic title that Paul Delvaux prepared for the Chaudfontaine fresco, a kind of allegory on the different ages of humanity, the train forms the link between the dawn of time and the unknown future. But the sequence is reversed—man leaves the universe he has created with the aid of science to return to the caves of his ancestors.*

If the artist's sole aim had been to convey to us this reflection on man's place in the universe, he would have limited himself to providing a purely narrative picture, leaving the onlooker, in his turn, to continue these disturbing meditations. But the artist here is concerned with far more than this and it is this deeper concern that we must examine.

As with all the explicit elements in his work, Delvaux portrays the train with only an apparent realism. The way in which he introduces this apparent realism into his message makes us perceive another reality, one which is only visible to the artist's inner sight. Delvaux paints the visible reality in order to escape from it. For in recounting this fable to us he is providing not a narrative but a poetic theme.

In this work, the train, a metallic insect with no soul, is constantly contrasted with all that is most tender, most secret and most fragile—the little girls who watch it in the light of the moon under a starless sky, the mysterious forest which enfolds it in its shadows as it stops at deserted stations. Taken separately, each of these elements indeed seems to belong to the world of visible reality. But the coming together of these elements, so different from each other and so violently opposed in the natural order of things, shatters the visible reality to reveal, to release the invisible, *whether sacred or profane, that only feeling can apprehend.*

The mere juxtapositioning of these contradictory elements would, however, not be enough to disturb us. We are disturbed and moved because, in the words of Malraux, "All expression divorced from the real is, in the last resort, poetry." Delvaux's old train leaves its metal carcase to become legend.

51. THE STATION

April 1971

Lithograph in black and white

Subject format: 57.5 × 78 cm
Paper format: 69 × 90.5 cm

One state only
Date on the stone, bottom right: 4-71

Lithographic crayon on transfer paper, transferred to stone

75 signed and numbered proofs on Arches paper
Stone polished out

The theme of the little girl lost in the solitude of unknown railway stations
has been used by the artist in several paintings:

Solitude, 1955 - S.H.W. No. 222; *Christmas Night*, 1956 - S.H.W. No. 223;
Night Train, 1957 - S.H.W. No. 231; *Local Line*, 1959 — S.H.W. No. 245;
Suburb, 1960 - S.H.W. No. 252; *Station in the Forest*, 1960 - S.H.W. No. 255;
Station at Night, 1963 - S.H.W. No. 280.

Ref. No. 44 of *Cahier Paul Delvaux No. 3*, B.L. pub., Paris, 1972 ➡

4-71

52 and 53. THE WINDOW

October 1971

Lithograph in two states
Subject format: 58 × 78 cm
Paper format: 68 × 93 cm

Date on the stone, bottom right: 10-71

No. 52: Black state.
  Lithographic crayon on transfer paper, transferred to stone
  50 signed and numbered proofs on Arches paper

No. 53: Colour state.
  The plate of the previous black state was used again by the artist
  as the background of this colour composition.
Each of the colours was transferred to zinc and superimposed on the black state.
  75 signed and numbered proofs on Arches paper

Stone polished out

52. THE WINDOW

N° 53 ➡

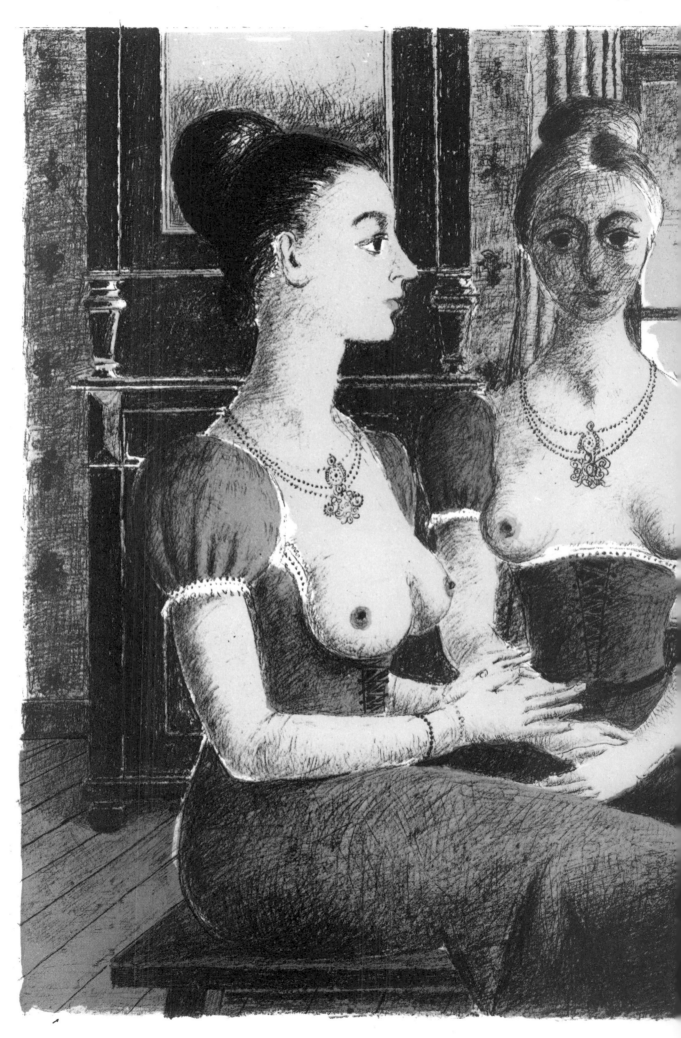

54. WOMAN WITH BALL

November 1971

Lithograph

Subject format: 49.5 × 31.5 cm
Arches paper format: 69.5 × 51.5 cm
Japan paper format: 69 × 51.5 cm

Date on the stone, bottom right: 11-71
Lithographic crayon on transfer paper, transferred to stone

75 signed and numbered proofs on Arches paper, printed in black
25 proofs printed in sanguine on Japan paper, signed and numbered
in Roman numerals
Stone polished out

Ref. No. 43 of *Cahier Paul Delvaux No. 3*, B.L. pub., Paris, 1972.
(The format is erroneously reversed)

November 1971

Black and white lithograph
Subject format: 32.5 × 69.5 cm
Paper format: 56 × 90 cm

One state only
Lithographic crayon on transfer paper, transferred to stone.
Date on the stone, bottom right: 11-71. Stone polished out.

Y

This composition was produced for the cover
of the *Cahier Paul Delvaux No. 3*, published on the occasion of the exhibition
"Graphic work 1969-1972" at the gallery *Le Bateau Lavoir*, Paris, February 1972
The central portion, format 20 × 45 cm,
of the lithograph was used for this cover
1,500 copies of the Cahier, format 20 × 16.5 cm, were printed

The theme of the tramway was often taken up by the artist,
in particular in the painting *Suburban Trains*, 1958, S.H.W. No. 241

56. THE FLAUTIST

January 1972

Lithograph in black

Subject format: 58 × 38.5 cm
Paper format: 71.5 × 51 cm

Date on the stone, bottom right: 1-72
One state only
Lithographic crayon on transfer paper, transferred to stone

75 signed and numbered proofs on Arches paper

Stone polished out

57. VANADÉ

January 1972

Lithograph in black

Subject format: 57.5 × 78 cm
Paper format: 68 × 90 cm

Date on the stone, bottom right: 1-72
One state only
Lithographic crayon on transfer paper, transferred to stone

75 signed and numbered proofs on Arches paper
Stone polished out

The theme of this plate was inspired by the "dialogue" being carried on at this time by the artist and the writer Alain Robbe-Grillet, the one expressing himself in pictures and the other in words, in preparation for the big illustrated book they were to produce jointly *Construction d'un Temple en ruine à la Déesse Vanadé (Building of a ruined temple to the goddess Vanadé).* The original edition of the book was published by the Bateau-Lavoir in April 1975 (cf Nos 81 to 91). ➡

58. SECRETS

To Fernand Mourlot

March 1972

Lithograph

Subject format: 31.5 × 24 cm
Paper, in the format of the book: 32 × 25 cm

Lithographic crayon on transfer paper, transferred to stone.
Date on the stone, bottom right: 15-3-72.
Created for Fernand Mourlot's book *Souvenirs et Portraits d'artistes*. Preface by Jacques Prévert, 1974.
800 copies of this book, format 32 × 25 cm, were printed. Each copy was signed by the author and numbered, 50 in Roman numerals.

This plate by Paul Delvaux is included in the book which also contains lithographs by many artists who have worked at the Mourlot workshops. Each artist provided a lithograph for the chapter devoted to him. None of the plates in the book are signed. Alain A.C. Mazo, Paris, and Léon Amiel, New York, pub., 1974.

The following additional, wide-margin proofs were printed:
45 signed and numbered proofs on Arches paper (47.5 × 35 cm).
25 proofs on Japan paper (47.5 × 35 cm), signed and numbered in Roman numerals.
15 proofs printed in sanguine on Japan paper (44.5 × 33 cm) signed and marked H.C. (*hors commerce* - not for sale).

Stone polished out

15-3-72

59 and 60. THE BEACH

June 1972

Lithograph in two states
Date on the stone: 6-72

No. 59: Black state.
Subject format: 58 × 78 cm
Paper format: 68 × 95.5 cm

Lithographic crayon on transfer paper, transferred to stone,
and printed on a light ochre background.

4 trial proofs without the ochre background
50 signed and numbered proofs on Arches paper

No. 60: Colour state.
Subject format: 58 × 78 cm
Paper format: 69 × 90.5 cm

The artist used the black of the previous plate as a background for the colours.
Colours on zincs

75 signed and numbered proofs on Arches paper
Stone polished out

N° 60 ➡

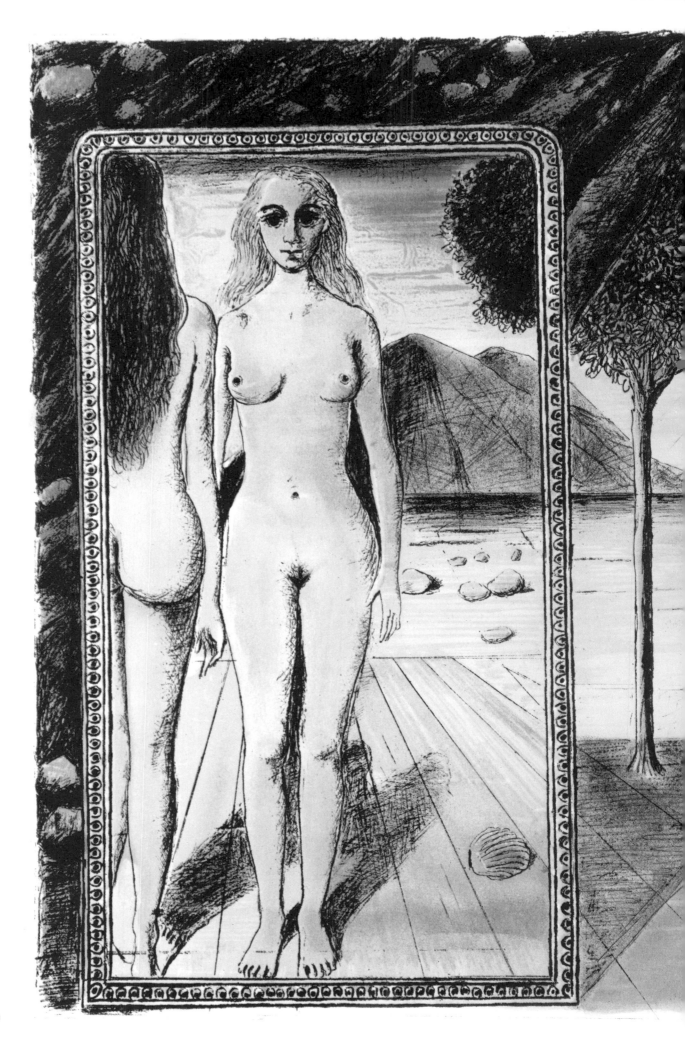

6-72

61. HAT 1900

January 1972
Lithograph in two states. Date on the stone, bottom right: 1-72
Black state - Formats: subject 59 × 39 cm; paper 72 × 50 cm
Lithographic crayon on transfer paper, transferred to stone
50 signed and numbered proofs on Arches paper

January 1972
Colour state - Formats: subject 59.5 × 39.5 cm; paper 73.5 × 50 cm
This colour state takes as a basis the plate of the previous black state. Colours on zincs.
75 signed and numbered proofs on Archer paper
Stone polished out

63 and 64. SILENCE

September 1972

Lithograph in two states
Date on the stone, bottom right: 9-72

No. 63: Black state.
Subject format: 59 × 78 cm
Paper format: 70 × 100 cm

Lithographic crayon on transfer paper, transferred to stone

50 signed and numbered proofs on Arches paper

No. 64: Colour state.
Subject format: 59 × 79 cm
Paper format: 68 × 100 cm

The artist used the previous black state as a basis
for this colour composition. Colours on zincs

75 signed and numbered proofs on Arches paper
Stone polished out

63. SILENCE

N° 64 ➡

65. THE DOLL

January 1973

Lithograph

Subject format: 31.5 × 24 cm
Arches paper format: 44 × 34 cm
Japan paper format: 44 × 34 cm

Crayon on transfer paper, transferred to stone
Date on the stone, bottom right: 1-73

75 signed and numbered proofs printed in black on Arches paper
25 proofs printed in sanguine on Japan paper,
signed and numbered in Roman numerals.

Stone polished out

65. THE DOLL

66. THE CAPTIVES

March 1973

Lithograph in black

Subject format: 79.5 × 58.5 cm
Paper format: 91 × 64.5 cm

Crayon on transfer paper, transferred to zinc
Date on the zinc, bottom right: 31-3-73
One state only
3 trials proofs in bistre

75 signed and numbered proofs on Arches paper

All the proofs of this edition bear the embossing stamp
of the gallery *Le Bateau Lavoir*, Paris. Zinc polished out. Grafolith printer.

66. THE CAPTIVES

Since October 1973, all editions have been made on paper bearing the watermark of the publisher, the Gallery *Le Bateau-Lavoir*, Paris, which is shown here. It is generally to be found at the bottom right of the sheet, though occasionally it can be seen in two parts, one half at the bottom right and the other half at the top left of the sheet.

67. THE VAULT

October 1973

Lithograph in two states

Subject format: 59 × 79 cm. Paper format: 71 × 93 cm

Date on the zinc: 10-73

No. 67: Black state.
      Lithographic crayon on transfer paper, transferred to zinc

50 signed and numbered proofs on Arches paper with the watermark of the B.L.

No. 68: Colour state
For the composition of this colour state the artist made use of the original black of the previous plate. A transfer to zinc was made for each of the colours which were then printed on the background of the black drawing.

75 signed and numbered proofs on Arches paper with the watermark of the B.L.
Zinc polished out

→

10-73

April 1974

Lithograph in two states.   Date on the zinc: 4-74.   Black and bistre states: Formats: subject
79 × 58.5 cm; paper 100 × 71.5 cm.   Lithographic crayon on transfer paper, transferred to zinc.
50 signed and numbered proofs printed in black on Arches paper with the watermark of the B.L.
35 proofs printed in bistre on Arches paper, with the watermark of the B.L., signed and
numbered in Roman numerals

70. THE CLAIRVOYANT

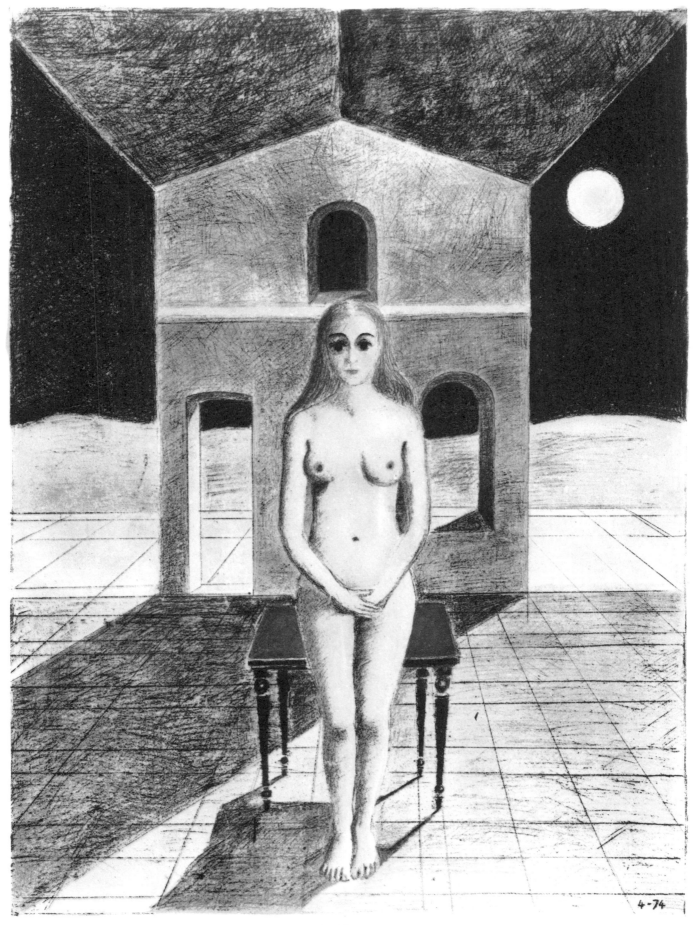

April 1974
Colour state - Formats: subject 79 × 58.5 cm; paper 100 × 68.5 cm
The black state was kept and used in this colour version. Colour on zincs
75 signed and numbered proofs on Arches paper with the watermark of the B.L. Zinc polished out

The same theme is taken up in the painting *The Sybille*, December 1973, S.H.W. No. 327.

July 1974

Lithograph in two states. Formats: subject 79 × 58.5 cm; paper 100 × 70.5 cm. Title and date: 7-74 in the plate, bottom right. Black and bistre states: Lithographic crayon on transfer paper, transferred to zinc. 50 signed and numbered proofs printed in black on Arches paper with the watermark of the B.L. 35 proofs printed in bistre on Arches paper with the watermark of the B.L., signed and numbered in Roman numerals.

July 1974

Colour state: same formats as the black state. To the previous black state the artist has added colours transferred to zincs. 75 signed and numbered proofs on Arches paper with the watermark of the B.L. Zinc polished out. The same theme appears in the painting *The Empress*, which was painted in the same year; reproduced in S.H.W. No. 330.

73. YOUNG GIRL WITH PEARL NECKLACE

January 1975

Lithograph

Subject format: 28.5 × 23 cm
Arches Paper format: 47 × 33.5 cm
Japan Paper format: 48.5 × 38.5 cm

Date on the plate: 1-75
Lithographic crayon on transfer paper, transferred to zinc.

45 proofs, printed in black, on Arches paper with the watermark of the B.L., signed and numbered in Roman numerals.

10 proofs were run off in sanguine, on Japan paper with the embossing stamp of the B.L. signed and numbered in Roman numerals.

100 signed and numbered proofs, printed in black, without margins, on Arches paper with the watermark of the B.L.

The 100 proofs without margins were inserted in the first 100 copies of the *Catalogue de l'Œuvre peint de Paul Delvaux*, by Susanne Houbart-Wilkins, with a preface by Michel Butor and Jean Clair, Cosmos pub., Brussels 1975.
Format of the book: 31.5 × 26 cm.

Zinc polished out.

74 and 75. PAÏOLIVE

April 1975

Lithograph in two states

Date on the plate, bottom right: 4-75

No. 74: Black state.

Subject format: 58.5 × 77.5 cm
Paper format: 71.5 × 90.5 cm
Lithographic crayon on transfer paper, transferred to zinc

75 signed and numbered proofs on Arches paper with the watermark of the B.L.

No. 75: Colour state.

Subject format: 59 × 78.5 cm
Paper format: 72.5 × 91.5 cm

To the black of the previous state the artist added the colours transferred to zincs
100 signed and numbered proofs on Arches paper with the watermark of the B.L.

Zinc polished out.

74. PAÏOLIVE

N° 75 ➡

4-75

Etching 29.5 × 21.2 cm

1971

Etchings
Text by Jacques Meuris

This book, format 39 × 29 cm includes plates of 5 full page etchings
by Paul Delvaux made between 1968 and 1971.

150 copies were printed on Rives B.F.K. paper
3 name copies

All the etchings are signed and numbered
Soleil Noir pub., Paris
Copper plates defaced

Etching 29.3 × 21.2 cm

Etching 29.3 × 21.2 cm

Etching 29.3 × 19 cm

Etching 14.5 × 11.5 cm

1971-1975

This book, format 44 × 55 cm, includes plates of 10 etching and one dry-point as the frontispiece (No. 81). They illustrate an original text by Alain Robbe-Grillet. Each etching accompanies one of the book's ten chapters.

This is how, in 1971, Robbe-Grillet described to the publisher the nature of the proposed collaboration with Paul Delvaux from which this book was to emerge. "The more I think about it the more certain I am that to achieve the inter-weaving of text and illustration you are aiming at, the most original and the most amusing method would be the form of dialogue I have suggested between the artist and the writer. I would write the first text and Delvaux would reply with an engraving (this would restate my theme, alter it, or suggest another one), I in turn would reply with another text, and so on up to ten engravings and texts. I would be very pleased if you could get him to agree to this unusual working method."

The method was adopted. The book was begun in 1971 but it took the artist, the author and the printer the four years up to April 1975 to complete it.

187 copies were printed on Arches wove paper with the publisher's watermark. These 187 copies were made up of:
30 copies numbered 1 to 30 with a set of prints on pale yellow-tinted Auvergne parchment, from the Richard de Bas paper-mill, with the publisher's watermark and signed by the artist.
120 copies numbered from 31 to 150.
30 copies *hors commerce* (not for sale) numbered from I to XXX.
5 name copies.
2 duty copies marked 0 and 00.

Each copy of the book bears the signature of the author and the artist on the page on which the number of the copy appears.

The following additional off-prints were made:
40 signed and numbered, wide margined proofs, format 49.7 × 64.7 cm, of each of the 11 engravings, on Auvergne parchment from the Richard de Bas paper-mill, white, bearing the publisher's watermark.
Crommelynck Printers.
Copper plates defaced.

Gallery Le Bateau-Lavoir, Paris, publisher.

Robbe-Grillet's text appeared the following year in a popular edition (Editions de Minuit), without illustrations, under the title *Topologie d'une Cité Fantôme*. Additional texts by the same author were inserted in the middle and at the end of the book.

81. FRONTISPIECE

Subject format: 26.7 × 35.7 cm. Paper format: 41.2 × 52.7 cm.

Plates 82 to 91: subject format 31.5 × 44.4 cm; paper format 41.2 × 52.7 cm.

82. IN THE CREATIVE CELL

83. OUTSIDE, THE SHADOWS LENGTHEN

84. STONE AND STILETTO

85. THE INSCRIPTION

86. THE SACRIFICIAL SHIP

87. ENTR'ACTE

88. THE HYPOTHETICAL BIRTH OF DAVID G.

89. THE ADJUSTMENT

90. THE HAPPENING

91. PRELIMINARY SKETCH FOR THE ENGRAVING

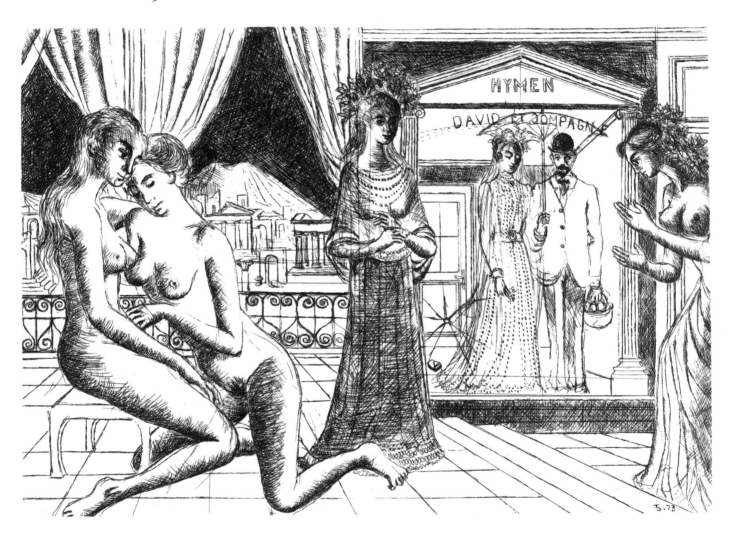

92. REFLECTION

December 1975

Lithograph in black

Subject format: 32 × 25 cm
Paper format: 50 × 39 cm

Lithographic crayon on transfer paper, transferred to zinc
Date on the plate, bottom right: 12-75
One state only

100 signed and numbered proofs on Arches paper with the watermark of the B.L.
Half these proofs have been inserted in the first 50 copies of this book.   Editions
André Sauret, Monte-Carlo and Rizzoli International, New York, pub.

This lithograph, without margins, forms the frontispiece of the standard version of
this book produced by the same publishers.   Format of the book: 32.5 × 24.5 cm.
5,000 copies of the book have been printed.   Zinc polished out.

93. THE SPEECH

December 1975

Lithograph in black

Subject format: 32 × 25 cm
Paper format: 50 × 39 cm

Lithographic crayon on transfer paper, transferred to zinc
One state only

100 proofs, signed and numbered, on Arches paper with the watermark of the B.L.
Half these proofs have been inserted in the first 50 copies of this book
Zinc polished out

93. THE SPEECH

December 1975

Lithograph in black. Subject format: 32 × 25 cm. Paper format: 50 × 39 cm. Lithographic crayon on transfer paper, transferred to zinc. One state only. 100 signed and numbered proofs on Arches paper with the watermark of the B.L. Zinc polished out.

December 1975

Lithograph in black. Subject format: 32 × 25 cm. Paper format: 50 × 39 cm. Lithographic crayon on transfer paper, transferred to zinc. Date on the plate, bottom right: 12-75. One state only. 100 signed and numbered proofs on Arches paper with the watermark of the B.L. Zinc polished out.

96. NAÏS CLOTHED

97. NAÏS UNCLOTHED

12-75

96. NAÏS CLOTHED

December 1975

Lithograph

Subject format: 32 × 11.2 cm
Arches paper format: 46.5 × 27.5 cm
Japan paper format: 46.5 × 27.5 cm

Lithographic crayon on transfer paper, transferred to zinc

90 signed and numbered proofs on Arches paper, printed in black,
with the watermark of the B.L.

2 trials proofs in sanguine on China paper with the embossing stamp
of the B.L.

15 proofs on Japan paper, with the embossing stamp of the B.L.
and run off in sanguine. Signed and numbered in Roman numerals.
Zinc polished out

97. NAÏS UNCLOTHED

December 1975

Lithograph

Subject format: 32 × 11 cm
Arches paper format: 46.5 × 27.5 cm
Japan paper format: 46.5 × 27.5 cm

Lithographic crayon on transfer paper, transferred to zinc

90 signed and numbered proofs on Arches paper, printed in black,
with the watermark of the B.L.

2 trials proofs in sanguine on China paper, with the embossing stamp
of the B.L.

15 proofs on Japan paper with the embossing stamp of the B.L. and
run off in sanguine, signed and numbered in Roman numerals. Zinc
polished out.

CONTENTS

THIS BOOK WAS PRODUCED BY EDITIONS
ANDRÉ SAURET. PRINTING WAS COMPLETED
IN AUGUST 1976 ON THE PRESSES OF THE
IMPRIMERIE MODERNE DU LION, PARIS.
THE ORIGINAL LITHOGRAPHS, FRONTIS-
PIECE AND DUST-COVER WERE RUN OFF
ON THE PRESSES OF FERNAND MOURLOT,
PARIS.